Holy Spirit Slingshots

Holy Spirit Slingshots

by Bill Laney & Andy Stirrat

HOLY SPIRIT SLINGSHOTS

Published by Slingshot Media LLC
PO Box 14951
Bradenton, FL 34280

© 2019 by **Bill Laney and Andy Stirrat**

Edited by Linda B. Bakonyi

Any websites referenced in this book as well as suggested reading are offered as resources and we are unable to endorse or vouch for content.

ISBN   9781708451615

Printed in the United States of America
First Edition 2019

DEDICATION

We dedicate this book to all those men and women who, knowingly or unknowingly, have contributed to each of our spiritual journeys.
These people have introduced us to God's story, the most profound love story on Earth. They have taught Sunday school, preached sermons, led small study groups, facilitated early morning men's prayer gatherings, recommended books and simply shown us their love in countless ways.

To all of them, we are grateful beyond words.

Bill and Andy

ACKNOWLEDGMENTS

We wish to thank for helping us with the writing, editing and publishing of this book:

Our wives, Sukie Laney and Marsha Stirrat, for their love, patience, support and suggestions toward the completion of this project.

Our friend and editor Linda B. Bakonyi for her tireless patience and help in making these stories readable.

All of the staff and volunteers at our church, Bayside Community Church of Bradenton, Florida, for spiritual guidance as well as advice and encouragement.

The Holy Spirit, for providing us and you, our readers, with stories of encounters and blessings that we can only begin to touch on here.

You, our readers, whom we thank you for reading this book. It is our sincere hope that you will be blessed by knowing   our   stories.

CONTENTS

Introduction What Is a Holy Spirit Slingshot?

1 Chapter 1 Coffee in the Convertible

3

Chapter 2 Book Beginnings

  10

Chapter 3 Rough Waters for the Maslin Family
  12

Chapter 4 Andy's Early Encounters with
  17   the Holy Spirit

Chapter 5 More Encounters with the Holy Spirit
  23

Chapter 6 He Values the Hair on Our Heads
  27

Chapter 7 Come Back

  33

Chapter 8 Sukie's Early Journey with the
42   Holy Spirit

Chapter 9 Importing Sukie from Tokyo

48

Chapter 10   Korean Adoptions
52

Chapter 11   How Sukie and I Got from   58
                Seattle to Bradenton

Chapter 12   Speaking in Tongues   63

Chapter 13   Some Selected Short Stories   70

Chapter 14   A Final Thought   84

Appendix A   Holy Spirit References   87

Appendix B   Q&A about Naltrexone & the   92
                Sinclair Method

Appendix C   Helpful Resources   98

What Is a Holy Spirit Slingshot?

Contributed by Bill & Andy

When we think of a slingshot, we often conjure up a vision of a kids' toy, Y-shaped and employing a rubber band of some type. Memories of shooting soda cans with pebbles fill our minds.

However, the slingshot we are using as our reference point is the one that David used when he defeated Goliath with a single shot to the forehead, using one of five smooth stones he had gathered in his shepherd's bag. The sling was probably made of leather. It would have had a pouch for the stone and two string handles, probably three feet long. He used the string handles to swing the stone over his head and then released the stone toward his target at just the right moment. Experts believe he delivered that blow with the force and accuracy of a well-aimed 38 revolver.

Each of the following stories describes encounters that we feel have the same accuracy and timing that only God could orchestrate. In every case, there is an overwhelming sense of presence that we believe is that of the Holy Spirit. As you read, you will realize the stories all involve people we have come to know through our church and small groups associated with it. It is our hope that some of these stories will strike a chord of recognition in you.

We are encouraged by the growth we see in our church and pray that growth will occur in Christianity worldwide. We have come to believe that the most explosive growth experienced in Christian communities today occurs in communities that recognize the truth of the Bible in its entirety. This includes the recognition that from the very beginning of creation, as recorded in the first chapter of Genesis, the Holy Spirit is present in every part of God's story.

As you read this book, our hope is that you will invite Holy Spirit to be a part of your life journey, making your story part of God's story.

CHAPTER ONE

Coffee in the Convertible

Contributed by Bus
As told by Bill

Bus Maslin and I first became friends when he joined a small group that my wife Sukie and I were hosting in our home as part of the life of Bayside Community Church in Bradenton, Florida. Our Lead Pastor Randy Bezet often says, "Life change happens in the context of relationships in small groups." I believe, dear reader, that the contents of this book will be a testimony in support of that.

The group was using the book *The God I Never Knew*, by Robert Morris, as a guide for a study of The Holy Spirit. This book, by the way, is one of the most powerful books I have ever read about the opportunity to have a friendship-type relationship with the Holy Spirit.

The participants in our group came from varied backgrounds and walks of life. The people in the early gatherings contributed the following:
- "I never heard about such a Spirit."
- "Is He some kind of a Spirit or Ghost as in Father, Son and Holy Ghost?"
- "Is He somehow a different part of the Trinity?."

- "It seems that most people connected to the Holy Spirit are doing weird things like speaking in tongues and I sure don't want to get involved in that."
- "Maybe he is God and, if so, I want to really get to know him!"

Bus fit into the last two categories. Even though there is a 25-year difference in our ages, we became good friends and developed a pattern of getting together for coffee a couple of times a month. During these meetings, his life story began to unfold before me.

Before moving to Bradenton, Bus was a top-producing sales engineer with an international technology company in Lexington, Kentucky. When offered a territory that included Florida, he jumped at the opportunity.

Over time, the increasing stress of Bus's work and his chaotic family life captured most of our coffee conversation. Our meetings became less frequent and I came to realize that Bus was an extremely high-functioning alcoholic.

One Friday afternoon, Bus sent a text asking me to meet him at Starbucks at four o'clock that same day. When I arrived, he already had coffee cup in hand and suggested that this was not a good day to sit outside and talk. On that day in Bradenton, Florida, lovebugs, small insects that hook up in tandem to mate, were everywhere in the air and would drive us crazy.

"Get some coffee and climb in the car; at least we'll be moving," Bus suggested. The top was down on his elegant, 2002 black Lexus convertible. My thinning white head made me patient #1 for the local dermatologists, because the brutal Florida sun puts me at risk of developing skin cancer. So, the hardtop came up and over and down and we were in a quiet cocoon, where Bus would be most comfortable driving and talking. We headed south on Anna Maria Island.

Bus began in a much more animated voice than his normal tech-sales-engineer's cadence. "I've known you, Bill, for five years and you, more than anybody else, know the struggles I've had with alcohol. One of the things I have truly appreciated about you is that you never talk down to me. You've never told me just to quit and you never dumped a lot of scripture on me." He reminded me of how he would beat himself up over his drinking and his failure to complete the "12 Steps" (A program of Alcoholics Anonymous, a recovery program for alcoholics).

"And since you haven't heard from me for the past couple of weeks, you probably aren't a bit surprised to learn that almost every night I've been slurping beer and bourbon to—I don't want to go there.

"A few days ago, when my head cleared up, I actually got a clear vision of how much my life was caving in, and if I didn't do something dramatic about my drinking, I would surely crash and burn. I began seriously researching residential rehab programs that utilize total abstinence, which may be the only option that would work for me. However, with the uncertainties of my job and having the kids from my failed marriage every other week, not to mention my ADHD, I just couldn't imagine how I would survive for 30 days in a 'cure center' somewhere."

He continued, "You may remember that when I was in your small group studying the book *The God I Never Knew*, I became acutely aware of what was happening to me with my first experiences in recognizing the remarkable gifts in my life that seemed to be orchestrated by the Holy Spirit, for which I am very grateful. But as time passed and the alcohol captured more and more of my life, the Holy Spirit's presence faded into the back crevices of my mind. However, a couple of nights ago, when I cried out to the Lord for help, He was there for me. The Holy Spirit was breaking through my muddled mind and urging me to look up alcoholism on the internet and to pay attention to what I found. I obeyed and what popped up was a video on YouTube, featuring a TED Talk recorded in London by a woman named Claudia Christian. I'd seen several TED Talks on Netflix and Amazon and I knew they had credibility, so I watched it. What she was sharing about her journey as an alcoholic was my story. I mean, she was absolutely describing me and all my struggles, and how I beat myself up and promised myself 'I'm not going to do it again.'

"For the first time, Bill, I saw hope in what Christian called the 'Sinclair Method.' So, I started looking into the Sinclair Method on the internet and I was unable to find anything that didn't support everything she said in the video. She even said that it had a 78 percent or more success rate. According to my research, the only side effect that might be experienced is a bit of stomach distress, or a headache or sleepiness."

At that point, Bus pulled over, reached behind my seat and pulled out his iPad. He opened it to the Sinclair Method YouTube video and handed it to me. I watched the whole presentation and so I could remember it, wrote down "Naltrexone", the drug used in the Sinclair Method.

I said to Bus, "This looks unbelievable to me, but just like you, I trust TED Talks to be well-vetted so there's got to be real truth here. Tell me Bus, what did you do?"

Bus said, "Fortunately, I have a long-term relationship with my doctor, so the very next morning, I called his office and asked for a prescription for Naltrexone as soon as possible. I got a return call and was told that I needed to see the office PA for an evaluation and was booked for 3 pm on that day. The appointment was a tough scene as the PA had never heard of Naltrexone and I think he must have figured that I was there to score some pain meds.

Finally, I said to him, "Listen, I'm doing everything right. I'm trying to recognize the fact that I have a problem. I called the office hoping to talk to my doctor and was told to come see you. So here I am and now you won't even talk to me about it.

"He told me to sit tight and he would talk to the doctor. So I sat there for almost an hour. When the PA came back, his demeanor had totally changed. He had researched Naltrexone and talked to the doctor and had a prescription already written. 'Ok', he said. 'Take one of these pills an hour before you're going to consume alcohol.' He continued his instruction with, '*Do not drink without taking the pill an hour ahead of time* and then come back in a month and tell us what you experienced. Make an appointment on your way out. This looks to me almost like a miracle drug.'

"So, 'script in hand, I hit a CVS drive-thru, with absolutely no idea of which pharmacies might have this drug or what it might cost. To my amazement and delight, CVS did have it, and with my company medical plan, my co-pay for a 30-day supply was only $26.57.

"Pill bottle in hand, I went home to take up my chores, including making dinner for the kids. It would be a while before I needed to start cooking, so I decided to take my first pill and lie down and rest for a bit. And, Bill, I woke up in about 30 minutes and literally thought I had been asleep for days. It felt like the most intense sleep I'd ever had. By then, it's only a half-hour before I can have my first drink of the evening; dinner can wait until I am properly fortified. But when I poured that drink and took the first gulp, there was no feeling like what I normally have. Euphoria was missing. I just held onto the glass from habit and it took me about three hours to finish it.

" Later, I poured a second glass, had a few sips and set it on the bedside table. It was still there when I came to in the morning. I realized for the first time in many months, that there was HOPE."

At that point, Bus and I had almost reached Starbucks. I said to him, "If what you have told me is true, and with this pill and the Sinclair deal you really get control over your drinking, there must be a ton of folks who would benefit from hearing your story. Maybe you ought to write a book."

Bus replied, "My answer to that crazy idea is, I could never write a book, but teaming up with you to write a book might be an idea worth thinking about. I'll be traveling for a couple of weeks. Let's pick up this conversation when I get back and see how I'm doing with the pill. We can talk over what the Holy Spirit might be saying to you about a book. I think he talks to you a lot more than to me."

CHAPTER TWO

Book Beginnings

As told by Bill

When we got together again, Bus reported that while on the two-week trip he had many business meals that included alcohol. He had faithfully taken his pill as prescribed and the alcohol began to taste like ginger ale. He never had more than one drink in an evening.

Bus had also decided that writing a book on top of his overloaded schedule was definitely out for him. However, always the sales guy, he had a proposal. If I would take on the task of writing the book, and if the focus were not on curing alcoholism, but experiencing the Holy Spirit for real; and if I were willing to open up and tell the story of my 50-year journey with the Holy Spirit, then Bus would sure appreciate a chance to contribute part of his story to the book.

Such a proposal, I was not expecting. As I began to chew on it, I realized that in the 50 years since I had been given a prayer language, I have experienced a joy that seems to bubble up whenever I use that language to sing and pray with the Holy Spirit. However, I never understood or acknowledged all of the other Holy Spirit gifts that were at play in my life. Maybe writing about some of these experiences would touch readers who were just like me, who have heard about the Holy Spirit over and over, but the "relationship" and "friendship" that are talked about were missing. And maybe, just maybe, the Holy Spirit might have a few folks from our local Bayside church family, who would show up to help me with the writing project. So I decided to give it my best shot and see what happens. I confessed to Holy Spirit that I felt like I was way over my head and asked Him to provide me with a partner to help me with the book.

The first person I thought of as a partner was my friend and fellow Bayside sojourner, Andy Stirrat. He had some experience with writing and publishing business-related books. We had already enjoyed many hours of sharing stories and experiences about our spiritual lives. I knew he loved the Lord and was in a sold-out relationship with the Holy Spirit. I outlined the project for him and told him how much I needed help. He wholeheartedly signed on and things we never imagined began to happen. Every time we felt like we knew where we were going with these stories, the Holy Spirit provided a new experience, a new story, a sermon; you get the idea. It was like the Holy Spirit was hitting with pin-point accuracy, much like David taking out Goliath with that smooth stone. Our hope is that you will come to understand why we like to refer to these instances as "Holy Spirit slingshots."

CHAPTER THREE

Rough Waters for the Maslin Family

Contributed by Bus
As told by Bill

Before I met Bus, he was an extremely busy guy, taking care of his clients; traveling for face-to-face meetings, or on his cell phone eight to ten hours a day, at home or in his car, or on the beach. At the same time, he was doing his best to function as a successful dad and husband.

Bus wanted to learn more about the Holy Spirit, who surely wasn't a ghost as he had been taught as a youngster, memorizing the Apostles' Creed about the Father, Son and Holy Ghost. Interestingly, our Pastor Randy Bezet recently gave a sermon about the role of the Holy Spirit. Part of his sermon was about getting to know the Holy Spirit and the myth that He is a ghost. Apparently, the Hebrew to English translation is responsible for this misinterpretation.

Bus signed up for a small group that my wife Sukie and I were leading and managed to get to most of the meetings. We were studying the book *The God I Never Knew* by Robert Morris. Bus was particularly intrigued by the discussions about the gifts of the Holy Spirit, especially the gift of miracles, as over the years he had experienced many instances where he now realized that God was providing just what he needed just when he needed it. It never occurred to him that the Holy Spirit residing in him might have been responsible for causing all these remarkable events, as needed.

About four years ago, two weeks before Christmas, Bus's then wife announced that she had talked with an attorney and was seeking a divorce. On top of that, the new owners of the company where he worked announced a major layoff and a freeze on all nonessential travel.

The good news is, he survived the layoff and with a travel ban, he was able to work from home, allowing him time to focus on his children and minimize for them the effects of the divorce.

To make life easier on the children, Bus and his departing wife came up with a plan to find a nearby one-bedroom apartment that could be rented month-to-month. Then, every other week, he or his wife would move to the apartment and the other would move back home with the kids, disrupting their young lives as little as possible.

Sure enough, two weeks later Bus found and moved into a delightful nearby one-bedroom apartment, rented month-to-month without a lease. The separation was underway. Another remarkable gift that came along with the apartment took place a day later, when he was returning to the apartment to pick up some documents. He was running late because of construction traffic and he was getting fully frustrated.

When Bus finally got to the apartment and parked, A man pulled in next to him. When he realized that Bus would be his new neighbor, he offered him some pizza. Bus declined the pizza, and the neighbor went on to offer Bus an almost brand-new couch and loveseat that he was about to donate to Goodwill. Amazed, Bus accepted the offer. With all the delays, Bus had arrived at the perfect moment. He called me later to let me know that he was beginning to believe that the Holy Spirit was involved in even the small stuff in our lives.

A few months later, the small stuff turned out to be a giant, never-to-be-forgotten miracle. Here's what happened: After the new rhythm of broken family life was up and running, Bus was at home with the kids late one Sunday afternoon, when he realized that they were out of insulin for their diabetic dog. He called the kids' mom and she agreed to come over to be with the kids while Bus went to a pharmacy to get the dog's insulin.

By the time the kids' mom arrived, the only open pharmacy was at Walmart. When Bus got to Walmart and discovered a long line at the pharmacy order window, he was feeling stressed. Under his breath, he was complaining to the Holy Spirit in no uncertain terms about what a rotten deal this was. After calming down, Bus noticed that the guy in front of him had an arm in a wing-type cast, and Bus spoke to him about it. The guy turned around and Bus noticed that he was wearing a realtor's shirt, which triggered a conversation about how the market was for family homes in West Bradenton. By the time the line had moved to the counter, the realtor had learned that Bus was going to have a five-bedroom house with a pool for sale as soon as he could get it cleaned up and ready to show, and it would be listed with one of his many realtor friends.

The guy in the cast said he understood all that, but he had a prospect from Connecticut who was in town this weekend looking for just such a home, and could he possibly break all the rules and take his client to the house right now? Bus thought, "What's going on here? Is this the Holy Spirit at work?" He paid for the insulin and told the guy to show up at the house in 45 minutes.

Forty-five minutes later, the realtor and his client were walking through the house, while the client was showing it to his wife on FaceTime. Later that night, the couple made a full-price offer with the provision that they could close and take possession in 30 days!

Later, going through the paperwork, the buyers agreed to do all of the cleanup and to pay the $4000 in needed repairs identified by a home inspector. In the meantime, Bus found two three-bedroom condos for rent in the kids' same school district and had everyone resettled in 29 days. If you had gone through that series of events, would you consider that just possibly, the whole deal could have been a Holy Spirit slingshot?

The Holy Spirit did not leave matters there. Four years later, Bus married a delightful, super-competent, beautiful woman by the name of Christy. A single mom of five added to the three who came with Bus, and they are raising eight children together.

Bus and Christy have launched a new business and Bus, no longer "employed," no longer has to travel. Bus is combining his technical skills and marketing knowledge with Christy's artistic side in their new, high-tech engraving business.

Most significantly, Bus has control over his drinking. As long as he continues to take his pill one hour before consuming any alcohol, he is able to enjoy a cold beer when fishing or working in the yard, with no worry of losing control. With that pill and Christy's love and support, the couple is free to focus on the critical role of the Holy Spirit in their life and the lives of their children. May God continue to bless them all.

For the convenience of any readers who have family friends, or who themselves are involved in alcohol addiction, we have included a Q&A section about Naltroxene and the Sinclair method in the Appendix.

—— CHAPTER FOUR ——

Andy's Early Encounter with the Unknown Holy Spirit

As told by Andy

The doctor handed me a tissue to wipe away the excess eye drops he used to dilate my eyes. He turned to my wife Marsha and said, "You need to encourage him to start working with a guide dog. Also, since you work with computers, Andy, you should start learning how to use a computer that works with speech commands. For all intents and purposes, in six months or less you will be blind. What you will see will be the equivalent of looking through a coke bottle."

I decided at that moment, if God wanted me to be blind, I would be the best blind guy around. I was also going to get a really cool smart dog to boot!

I had just recently been diagnosed with glaucoma. This disease runs in my family and is the type based on the shape of the eye. I had lost half the vision in my left eye about 15 years earlier. When the glaucoma specialist tested my range of vision, he came back with the alarming news that not only did I lack 50 percent of the vision in my left eye; the test indicated I was also rapidly losing vision in my right eye.

Thus began my journey through every vision test known to medicine at the time. Every type of eye specialist was consulted; blood tests for metals were performed, because I worked in a factory environment. Who knew there were so many types of ophthalmologists?

Each time I would return to my glaucoma doctor, the news was grim. I was continuing to lose my vision.

Once the doctor suggested that I work with a dog, Marsha and I proceeded to do a lot of the things you do when you know you are losing your vision. I was young, about to turn 50, with grandchildren in my future and a lot of other people and places I wanted to be able to see.

Marsha and I maxed out our credit cards visiting my hometown and childhood home; visiting her hometown and childhood home; taking cruises and visiting children who lived out of state. In short, I was capturing visual memories.

As far back as I can remember, I have always had a strong faith in God and I trusted that whatever His will was, that was what I wanted too. My paternal grandmother had gone blind from glaucoma before my father was born and her faith was unshakeable.

Raised in a Christian home, my family lived around the corner from the local Methodist church that my mother attended when she was a teenager. If the doors were open, my family was there. Even when church was not in session, my dad and I could be found taking care of the old building and its grounds. The church was built in the 1890s and there was a parsonage next door. My dad taught industrial arts in the local high school and so had adequate knowledge and skills to maintain these old buildings.

Never doubting that I was a Christian, I eagerly attended confirmation classes at age 12. I accepted Jesus Christ as my personal Savior and declared before my church, family and peers that I would obey His commands and live a life worthy of His sacrifice.

However, by the time I was 14, I was already compromising my values. I had discovered beer and the opposite sex. Early one morning I woke up unable to move. I had enjoyed partying with friends the night before. Not only was I feeling the effects of too many beers, I was also suffering from a severe backache from the chicken fights we had enjoyed in the pool. Chicken fighting involved having a girl on your shoulders wrestling with a girl on another guy's shoulders. The first couple to go under the water lost. I had enjoyed quite a few victories with a rather plump young lady, who happened to look very good in a swimsuit. I suspect the beers made me unaware of how much stress this was putting on my back. I woke up literally unable to move. I remembered my pastor telling us that prayer would help us overcome any obstacle. So I prayed.

As I prayed, I felt a warmth come over me. It was similar to the way an instant chill overtakes you, only it was warm. My back was instantly healed. At that time in my life I knew who God was and was reasonably sure I knew Jesus, but I was pathetically clueless about the Holy Spirit. I remember as a young boy asking my mom who the Holy Ghost was, since we didn't believe in ghosts. I got a vague answer that was along the lines of: Jesus, after the resurrection, came back as a ghost. In fairness, I was very young at the time and may have misunderstood her answer. Suffice it to say, my Methodist upbringing had some liturgical references to the Holy Ghost in the Apostles' Creed, Gloria Patri and Doxology, but the Holy Spirit was definitely not part of the Sunday school or sermon teachings.

It was not until 30 years later that I became formally introduced to the Holy Spirit. My diminishing played an integral part in this.

While dealing with my loss of sight, Marsha and I had become frustrated with the Methodist church we were attending. We were most concerned for our teenage children who were being taught nothing about Christian doctrine.

We found an Assembly of God church with an extraordinary youth group with almost 1,000 students. The youth ministry was well organized, with a weekly Wednesday evening service that focused on the Bible and small groups. Our kids loved it.

Having developed professional-quality audio-visual skills, I became the person who was responsible for sound, lighting and slideshow for Wednesday night adult services. On one particular Wednesday there was a healing service. The woman facilitator gave general invitations: "Anyone who is experiencing back pain, come forward and be healed; anyone who is suffering from cancer, come forward and be healed; anyone who has been told they need a knee replacement...."

Groups of people went forward and we all prayed over them. Many of them claimed instant healing. Then she said, "There is a man in the room who has an eye infection. He has been told he will go blind. The doctors cannot figure out what is wrong. God has told me He does not want this man to be blind and if that man will come forward, He will heal him." Marsha urged me to go forward and even though I could not imagine the doctors would have missed an infection, I went. More than 100 people laid hands on me, praying in tongues. As they prayed over me, I experienced that familiar warmth, like a warm chill. Now, as I look back, I can clearly remember the same warmth that came over me as a teenager, and I was finally able to identify that feeling as the presence of the Holy Spirit.

Soon after, I returned to the glaucoma doctor's office for another round of testing. When the tests were over, the doctor gave Marsha and me shocking news. "We have performed every test we know to perform and had you see every kind of specialist. Yet, we have been unable to determine why you were losing vision so rapidly. I'm even more baffled now because it seems your vision has improved and is almost back to normal, which is medically impossible."

When I told the doctor about my experience at the healing service and how 100 or more people I didn't know had laid hands on me and prayed in tongues, he replied "That must be it, because I have been praying for you also."

To this day, I can be in a grocery store in the town where we lived at that time, and someone who was in the group praying for me that night will come up to me, and we will stop on the spot and thank God for what he gave me. I now know it was the Holy Spirit who was doing the healing, and the whole experience is surely one of those Holy Spirit slingshots in my life.

CHAPTER FIVE

More Encounters with the Holy Spirit

As told by Andy

Once I became aware of Holy Spirit's presence in my life, I came to realize that those warm chills I had experienced many times before and since were actually reminders that He is ever-present in my life.

Several years after my sight was rescued, I had the opportunity to experience a "slingshot" with my dad. Dad was probably the most significant influence in my Christian walk. While he rarely spoke of his faith, it was evident in his actions and in how he lived his life.

When my mom was no longer able to care for herself because of early-onset Alzheimer's, Dad's faith was apparent in the way he patiently took care of her. When my siblings and I would try to convince him to get help or put her in assisted living, he would refuse and tell us it was what he wanted to do. I would watch him spend the first hour of the day meticulously making breakfast for Mom, then for his boxer Buddy and then for himself. Often Mom would also eat Dad's breakfast while he was still preparing it. By then, it was time for lunch, and he would start all over.

My sister had given my dad a copy of *The 36-Hour Day* by Peter Raebins and Nancy L. Mace. It's a self-help guide for caregivers of people with dementia, Alzheimer's and other neurological disorders. I remember noticing it was well-worn with many sticky-note placeholders.

One day, I got a call from my sister-in-law, telling me that my mom had been transported by ambulance to the ER. It was unclear if Mom had had a heart attack or a stroke. I flew down immediately from Dallas to find my dad struggling to keep my mom from yanking out her IVs. She was in a state of agitation.

A therapist came in to determine if Mom could swallow food and perhaps feed herself. She was unable to do either and I said to my dad, "Your 36-hour day just became a 72-hour day." At my urging and with the insistence of Mom's doctor, Dad and I went looking at facilities that provided memory care.

Mom had a tendency to wander, so some facilities were crossed off the list as there was no way to keep patients inside. One would have been fabulous, but for the fact that it was located on the third floor with no way to keep patients out of stairways. The facility we liked the most had 18 beds and required entering a code to unlock the door to enter or leave the memory care section. In addition, it was immaculately clean and always had a staff of four to take care of and monitor the patients. We were impressed with the way the staff interacted with the patients and with the activities they engaged in with them.

The best part was that the facility was just a few blocks from my dad's house and he could drive there safely in just a few minutes. The bad part was that there was a five-year waiting list.

We ultimately decided to put Mom in the rehab part of this facility and continue to pursue a long-term memory care solution. We were assured she would have an ankle bracelet that would sound an alarm and automatically lock any exit door she came close to.

It was hard to get Mom in and out of the car even on one of her good days, so I convinced Dad it would be best to hire a wheelchair ambulance to move her to the rehab facility. He could show up there afterwards and calm her down as she adjusted to her new surroundings. We were told that would happen later on the same day, so we went back to my dad's house to clean his yard. A tropical storm had come through a few days earlier and left a mess. After Dad and I left the hospital Mom was moved to the new facility.

While raking leaves and clearing branches, Dad asked, "Do you believe God still does miracles like he did in the Bible?" I told him I did and shared with him how God had healed me from my 35-year tobacco addiction after I prayed about it. I also told him about the Holy Spirit encounter with my eyesight. He got really excited.

When we went to check on my mom, she was being evaluated by a physical therapist to determine how much rehab she would need. The therapist relayed to us that she was totally uncooperative, and he needed more time as she wouldn't get up so he could see if she could walk. He asked us to come back in an hour. As we turned to leave, I felt that familiar warm chill come over me—my mom had gotten up from the wheelchair and followed my dad. As the therapist walked along with us, evaluating my mom's ability to walk, we ran into the facility administrator who asked my dad if we had considered their memory care wing. My dad replied we were interested but didn't think we could wait for five years. The administrator told us that once Mom had become a patient of the facility, she automatically went to the top of the list and they had just had an opening come up. But we needed to decide right then. I looked Dad in the eye and said, "There's your miracle, Pop!"

"There's your miracle Pop"

What we did not know at the time was that my dad, who was in excellent health, would have a fall within a few months that would ultimately prove to be fatal. Had the Holy Spirit not performed this "slingshot," I don't believe my mom would have had such a good outcome. She got the care she needed in the facility that was best suited to her needs when she needed it most.

CHAPTER SIX

He Values the Hair on Our Heads
Marsha's Story

Contributed by Marsha
As told by Andy

It was date night and Marsha and I had just enjoyed a great dinner. As we were driving home, I pulled into an auto dealership to look at the interior of a car that had recently been introduced. As we stepped out of our car, we felt the beginnings of fall on a windy Texas evening. As the wind struck her face, Marsha felt an intense toothache come on and we decided to forgo looking at the car in favor of returning to our warm car and heading home.

The following morning, the toothache had not gotten any better so she went to our dentist. An examination and x-rays did not reveal any reason for Marsha's pain so she was referred to a local endodontist to see if a root canal were needed. Using dry ice, the endodontist was unable to find a reason for Marsha's pain. She was sent home with a screaming toothache and a prescription for painkillers.

Our Sunday school teacher and good friend Ron was running for mayor of the town we lived in. Days later, Ron was hosting his campaign kickoff at a local Lions Club meeting hall and was serving catered barbecue. Marsha and I absolutely love barbecue and we are quite fond of

Ron, so even though Marsha was still in excruciating pain, we went to the party.

In addition to being an awesome Sunday school teacher as well as an aspiring mayor, Ron was also an emergency room physician. He would drive about four hours from the Dallas area to the Shreveport, Louisiana, area and be on duty for three days at a time.

When Marsha and I got to his campaign party, we apologized to Ron because we would not be able to stay, but told him that we would contribute to his campaign and take home some yard signs. We were headed to the local ER to see if it might have a dentist on call to get some relief for Marsha. Ron asked Marsha to describe her pain. When she did, Ron told her to tell the doctor at the ER that she was suffering from Tic douloureux.

We headed to our local hospital and told the resident on duty at the ER what our friend Ron told us to say. The doctor told us to wait in the exam room; he would get back to us in a while. Marsha and I were pretty sure the doctor thought we were hoping to get some good drugs. We were equally sure he had never heard of Tic douloureux.

It was evident when the doctor returned that he had either consulted a medical dictionary or Google as he proceeded to educate us about trigeminal neuralgia, which is a severe, stabbing pain on one side of the face. He explained that the trigeminal nerve is the nerve that supplies sensation to the face. Trigeminal neuralgia is a condition in which blood vessels press on this nerve and it is considered one of the most painful conditions that can affect people. Tic douloureux is the Cajun name for this condition.

The ER doctor referred us to an ear, nose and throat doctor. When Marsha went to see this doctor, he confirmed the diagnosis and said that this was one of the worst conditions to have and he was sorry but nothing could be done for her. She left his office weeping and believing this would be her new normal forever.

We did some research on trigeminal neuralgia and found a neurosurgeon who specialized in the condition. After speaking with Marsha, he assured us we had been truly blessed with an early diagnosis. Most people have teeth removed and go through a myriad of tests before it is diagnosed correctly. The surgeon said there were surgical options; however, his recommendation was to try an anti-seizure medication first. The medicine and prayers from our Sunday school class and small groups (which the doctor had not thought to prescribe) were effective. When we returned for follow-up with him, Marsha was no longer experiencing pain.

To confirm his diagnosis, the surgeon ordered an MRI to ensure there was nothing else going on. While in the tube, the technician accidentally left his microphone open and Marsha overheard him say, "We'll have to get a few more pictures, that looks like a tumor."

As you can imagine, we were alarmed. When we returned to the surgeon to get the MRI results, he told us it was a meningioma and assured us that it was not a serious one unless it started to grow. Apparently, many people who have this type of brain tumor never even find out unless they have other reasons to have an MRI. He referred us to a neurologist who would monitor the tumor, and over the next few years, Marsha would have an MRI every six months to ensure there was no growth.

One of the MRIs revealed significant growth. In addition, Marsha was experiencing headaches and other indications that something was not right. Marsha's neurologist recommended she have the surgery right away to avoid the risk of seizures and other problems. I asked him whom he would send someone he loved to. My question irritated him, but he reluctantly told me that the doctor he would use thought he was God and knowing of our faith and love for Jesus, we probably wouldn't like him. We asked him to recommend a Christian neurosurgeon who specialized in brain surgery. He recommended we talk to Dr. Barnett, head of neurosurgery at Baylor Hospital in Dallas.

When we met Dr. Barnett, one of Marsha's first questions was, "Do you consider yourself a real Christian? I mean, not just on Sunday?" He assured us that he was very involved with his faith. He was still prayer partners with his college roommate and they routinely got together to pray with one another.

As we were driving home after scheduling surgery with Dr. Barnett, I received a phone call from one of Marsha's very close Mary Kay friends, Marianne (Marsha is a Mary Kay Sales Director). She said, "Oh my gosh, Andy, I was on a prayer call this morning with my Mary Kay prayer partners and we prayed for Marsha. I just heard that she will have to have brain surgery. Do not talk to anyone else; my husband's prayer partner since college is the head of neurosurgery at Baylor, his name is Dr. David Barnett."

Talk about a Holy Spirit slingshot! It gets even better. One of Marsha's questions for Dr. Barnett was, "Do you really have to shave my head?" He assured us that this was a routine matter and that it avoided complications. Marsha's closest friends threw her a scarf party so she would be able to cover her wound and missing hair, and she must have received more than 100 beautiful scarves.

The night before her surgery, Marsha asked if I would help shave her head before she "died" tomorrow. I assured her she was not going to die and that God would watch over every aspect of her surgery and her hair would grow back fine before she knew it.

Right before going into the OR, Dr. Barnett joined Marsha and me and our family and prayed with us. His prayer included asking God to join him and his team and to help guide them through a successful surgery. The surgery lasted exactly two hours, as Dr. Barnett had said it would. He came out to tell me that all went perfectly. He believed pathology would show absolutely no cancer and he was confident Marsha would recover with no complications whatsoever. Hallelujah! As he turned to walk off, Dr. Barnett stopped and said, "God told me to leave her hair alone so I made a quarter-inch part for my incision. She will be able to comb over it and no one will ever see it."

As you can imagine, Marsha was ecstatic to learn she got to keep her hair. For her, this was her miraculous Holy Spirit slingshot. When we returned for surgical follow-up, the PA took us aside and said, "I don't know what you told the doctor but I want to thank you; Doctor Barnett has allowed me to do that same part for every surgery we have done since and it means so much to our teenage patients."

Marsha was able to answer, "It wasn't me who told him – it was God!"

CHAPTER SEVEN

"Come Back"

Contributed by Evy
As told by Andy

I woke up in a hospital room wondering why I was there. My mom was sitting next to the bed, looking worried. I felt woozy, as if medicated. I asked,
"Why are we here?"
"You had a seizure and the doctors are trying to determine why."
"How long will I have to be here?"
"We won't know until the doctor comes back. In the meantime, I   want to talk to you about our plans."

I had a feeling I wasn't going to like what I was about to hear but I felt too weak to argue. I had obviously been medicated and felt as if I could fall asleep any second.
I asked, "Can this wait until we get home?"
"Your father has bought a home for us in Puerto Rico and we will be moving there very soon. You can come with us or stay here. It is up to you."

As my shocked brain took this in, questions started, slowly at first, then in a torrent:

- I'm only 16. Who will take care of me?
- Where will I live if I stay?
- How will I live if I stay?
- If I go, will I ever see my friends again?

- What about school?
- What about this seizure I've had and future medical issues?

As my mind went through all of these things, I realized I had only once felt this vulnerable and scared in my life. Remembering what happened, I acquiesced and said, "When will we be moving?"

My earliest childhood memories are of feeling like a princess. My Daddy doted on me as I was the only child for the first ten years of my life. My Daddy was easy to anger, so I was always careful to be Daddy's girl.

We lived in New York City, in the Bronx and until I was five, I thought everyone was Puerto Rican. Where we lived, Puerto Ricans were the only people I ever saw. I was raised around my many cousins and was pleasantly shocked to find a cultural diversity of children when I first entered Kindergarten.

The Bronx in the early '60s was a local epicenter of immigration. Until I started school, I was mostly isolated from other children, except for my cousins, and I was quite surprised at the large number of kids in my school.

Speaking of cousins, I got to know one of them in a way that no eight-year-old girl ever wants to know her teenage male cousin. This was what made me feel so vulnerable and scared when my mom told me about moving to Puerto Rico. I didn't know what it was called but when I told my mom about what had happened, she said, "Do not tell your father. He will kill your cousin and go to jail. We will never see him again."

I didn't want to lose my Daddy so I held it in. I couldn't help feeling let down and unprotected but knew it was for the best. Not surprisingly, when, after nearly 50 years, I finally shared this rape experience with my dad, his response was, "I'll kill him!"

Now I have come to see the beauty in my dad, as he is taking care of my ailing mother and is devoted to my sisters. In addition, he is a hard-working, hard-gambling, beautiful man.

When I was ten, my mom had a baby and I gained a little sister. When I was 14, she had another baby and now I had two sisters. As both my parents worked, I was responsible for my sisters' care. I am ashamed to say I was ill-equipped for this task and often resorted to hitting them. I am thankful that today they do not hold it against me and I know they love me, as I love them dearly.

During this period, my father doted on us girls but often complained about not having a son. I had enjoyed being the only apple in my father's eye for ten years, and I began trying to get his attention and affection by becoming more like a son to him. The more I tried however, the more distant he became.

When we moved to Puerto Rico the school I went to there was much stricter than the one I had attended in the Bronx. Comfortable jeans and polo shirts were replaced by stiff uniforms and new rules. Less than two weeks later, I informed my mom that I would no longer be attending school. Instead, I would work to receive my G.E.D. I think my mom knew at this point, she could not force me to continue in school.

A bright spot in my life at this time came from my father's sister who invited me to attend church with her. Prior to this, I have no recollection of attending church. My aunt was a member of a Pentecostal church and this is where I became familiar with the Holy Spirit. I welcomed the Holy Spirit into my life and learned to recognize His voice. I made a few friends at church and when they decided to attend a Pentecostal Bible school, I decided to go with them. There, I met a fellow student named Elva.

Elva was ten years older and married, with three children. We quickly became best friends. Elva invited me to visit her home and we became lovers. Shortly after that, we dropped out of Bible school and, in essence, stiff-armed the Holy Spirit. It would be many years before I would hear His voice again.

Elva told me I satisfied her better than her husband ever had and she urged me to move in with her. At this point in my life, I was hungry for the relationship, so I moved in. For a time I lived with Elva, her husband, and their three children. Needless to say, this caused conflict in Elva's marriage, and her husband moved in with his mother and ultimately divorced Elva.

We continued to live in the house for a year or so until it was sold, and Elva and her ex split the proceeds. Elva and I enrolled in Central University of Bayamón and later got part-time jobs. My area of study was physical education with a concentration on special needs. Elva enrolled too and majored in special ed. Eventually financial and family stress were too great and I dropped out, while Elva continued her studies.

From time to time, Elva would bring up the conflicts between our lifestyle and our faith. We both tiptoed around unspoken issues. In retrospect, I realize that the enemy uses the flesh to confuse us, even when we know that what we want is not always the way things are supposed to be.

Gradually my relationship with Elva began to deteriorate. The original happiness we had enjoyed with one another began to turn into periods of anger and silence. Elva began to put me down in front of the children. I remember a time when Elva's 12-year-old said to me, "Don't worry, we still love you." When Elva's family members would visit, she kept me hidden. She introduced me to her friends as a cousin who was living with her.

During this period Elva's family and I moved to Florida, and we struggled to raise the kids in a poverty household. As time went by our relationship continued to deteriorate. Seventeen years after it began, Elva finally decided her relationship with Christ was too important and she had to leave me to please God. She wistfully shared with me, "I could have stayed if you were a man, but as long as you are still a woman, we cannot be together."

After Elva, I had several other lesbian relationships. The first one did not last very long. The second lasted for five years and we are still friends today. It is more like a close friendship than a sexual relationship.

About ten years ago, I met a man through an internet match site who had transitioned to a woman. We agreed to meet at a local restaurant and he told me, "You're a man." He suggested I go through the transition process to become a man.

That man gave me the name Evan. Using hormone therapy, I went through the process of transitioning and legally changed my name as well as gender. I began dressing and living as a man. For the next eight years I lived alone and had a few one-night stands.

One night, while staying up and watching my favorite show on TV, "Saturday Night Live," I heard a familiar voice from 40 years ago. It was the Holy Spirit saying,
"Come Back."
I replied, "I can't; I'm too far gone."
"Come Back," the Holy Spirit repeated.
"You're not going to forgive me"
"Come Back."
"I have done too many things...."
"Come Back."

I struggled with His invitation for the rest of the night and finally decided to obey and said, "Yes." In the morning, I called my youngest sister who is a strong believer and told her, "Something happened." My sister listened and gave me the phone number of her church. I called the pastor and it was as if it were a miracle from God. The pastor assured me, "If He hadn't already forgiven you, you would not be talking to me."

That wonderful pastor invited me to come to his church. It was in Fort Lauderdale, but I live more than four hours away in Bradenton. He suggested I try a church of the same denomination where I live in Bradenton. I called a nearby church and left a message, but my call wasn't returned. Then, I tried a church in Sarasota. The pastor there graciously came to my home to meet with me. I felt welcomed by him, but not necessarily by his church. Understanding my desire to return to my faith as well as my gender, he recommended that I get Christian counseling. I followed his advice and met with such counselors several times. The counselors did not understand that gender transition is not a decision that can be implemented immediately; it's a lengthy process.

Frustrated, I did an internet search to see if I could find additional help and support and discovered Global Media Outreach, an internet organization dedicated to bringing Jesus to everyone. I filled out a form and the next day, a lady named Anneta called me. For the next two weeks she called me every day. After learning my story, Anneta introduced me to Denise Shick, director of *Living Stones Ministries* and *Help for Families Ministries*. These are websites for families dealing with sexual identity issues. The mission of Living Stones Ministries is to help individual homosexual, transgender or other sexually broken people. The mission of Help for Families is to help families and their loved ones who are impacted by homosexuality or transgenderism. Denise Shick was totally understanding and extremely helpful, even to the point of calling me every week.

Denise introduced me to a professional counselor named Mark, a psychotherapist who connected me with Bayside Community Church in Bradenton. For the first time in decades, I again felt welcome and loved in a church and had found a new home.

Bayside Community Church offers open enrollment in small groups several times a year. I signed up for a small group that was going to study a book called *The God I Never Knew,* by Robert Morris. The group was meeting in the home of Bill and Sukie Laney. Spending additional time in study with Bill and Sukie has encouraged me to dig deeper into my faith. As I continue to study God's Word and get more deeply involved in the church, I have come to realize God's unconditional and unfailing love for me. Contrary to what the transgender community holds, I do not believe God made a gender mistake while I was in my mother's womb. I am firmly convinced that restoration begins with Jesus on the Cross.

> *"I do not believe God made a gender mistake while I was in my mother's womb. "*

Andy's take:

Now Evy is well on her way to following the Holy Spirit's invitation. Fortunately, she never went through surgical changes. Under medical supervision, she is slowly reducing the hormones that give her a male appearance.

Unfortunately, because she has epilepsy, the possibility of having a seizure requires that she be weaned off of the medicines slowly.

Evy has completed paperwork to change her name and has gone before a judge to finalize the process of legally reclaiming her original name Evelyn and her gender.

Evy was also recently baptized. With the help of her doctors, her church and the friends she has found there, as well as her friendship with Denise Shick, her transition will soon return Evy to her God-given gender as female.

CHAPTER EIGHT

Sukie's Early Journey with the Holy Spirit

Contributed by Sukie
As told by Bill

Have you ever wondered about the phrase some people casually throw around, "God has a plan for your life?" In his Book, *Blue Like Jazz*, Donald Miller manages to condense the "plan" God has for us into these three profound guidelines.

God simply says,

- "Write a good story of your life by the   decisions you make day by day."
- "Take a companion with you"
- "Let Me help you!"

My wife Sukie Laney is the personification of these three guidelines.

This is my take on how Sukie has been writing a good story of her life, given the decisions she has made and how she has taken me as her companion along the way, and how she has quietly leaned into the Holy Spirit to help her.

Sukie was born in Tokyo in 1946, into a fractured family that had survived the Second World War. She lived in a traditional Japanese house in the heart of Tokyo, with a brother who was ten years older, a sister who was 11 years older, an absentee business-owner father, her mother, and, at times, an elderly aunt and uncle. There were no bedrooms; they all slept on mats on the floor. Sukie felt like an only child growing up. Post-war Japan had a youth culture focused on education, education, and more education, six days a week, twelve hours a day including subway time.

When Sukie finished high school, she learned about a small two-year girls' college in downtown Tokyo. It had a good reputation, and she convinced her father to let her enroll. This college had been established more than 100 years earlier by the Canadian Methodist Church and old Bibles were still being used as textbooks. In the college, learning to be a proper Japanese lady, she was given one of those well-worn old Bibles and an introduction to someone named Jesus. At this point in her life, what she was learning had no impact on her Buddhist beliefs.

Finishing school, Sukie met an American electronics inventor who was a follower of Jesus. They fell in love and married. Her new husband brought her to America, where they settled in Billings, Montana—a far cry from the streets of Tokyo. Within a year, she had lost both a preemie baby and her husband, when he died during back surgery.

In the midst of her grief and loneliness, one afternoon while standing in her yard, Sukie had an encounter with the Holy Spirit. This is how she tells it: "As I stood there with the garden shears in my hand, I cried out in my pain, 'Lord, if

you are real, I want to know.' All of a sudden everything seemed to stop. A silent peace flooded the garden. I seemed to hear, 'Yes I'm real and everything will be all right for you. Trust me.'
I knew it wasn't Buddha!"

"I knew it wasn't Buddha!"

After that encounter, Sukie began to read her late husband's Bible. And when she read it, she simply believed it, all of it—unlike me when I first read the Bible.

In due course, with an introduction from a neighbor, Sukie called the local Methodist pastor, told him what had happened to her, and asked him to baptize her. He agreed and Sukie settled into that church community and began to grow in the Methodist doctrine and worship style.

Sukie also got a job as an aide in a nursing home and signed up for English classes, which ultimately led to a job in the athletic department of the University of Montana.

Along the way, Sukie began to realize that what she was experiencing in the church just didn't match up with what she was reading in her Bible and she began to pull back. At that point, through what almost seemed to be orchestrated encounters, she began to meet people who were telling her about their experiences with baptism in the Holy Spirit. Her curiosity began to grow to the extent that when she heard about a gathering of Spirit-filled folks taking place in Bozeman, she decided to go, even though it was a six-hour drive when it wasn't snowing!

"I got there right at dinnertime and I was graciously welcomed and offered a meal. After dinner and some wonderful worship music, the participants began to share their experiences, and I started asking questions and more questions. Finally, one of the leaders said to me, 'Sukie, you didn't drive all this way over the mountains just to ask a bunch of questions, did you?' I said no. He said, 'Would you allow us to lay hands on you and ask the Holy Spirit to give you a prayer language?'

"I said yes, and they prayed for me. But I guess I was so proud that I just couldn't turn my voice over to some strange spirit, even if it was holy. Nothing happened until I got back in my car and started the drive home.

"I opened my mouth to pray for safe travel and out came a stream of beautiful words. It was my prayer language! I sang and prayed in that language all the way back to Billings, and it has never left me since."

Not only did Sukie's prayer language never leave her, but back in Billings, as she got connected with other Spirit-filled believers, she became part of the leadership team in Montana for what came to be known as the Charismatic Renewal Movement.

This was a season of spiritual renewal across America, sparked by St. Luke's Episcopal Church in Seattle. Many folks in the First Methodist Church in Billings received a prayer language, among them, the youth pastor and his son. The same thing was happening in other churches in town, including among Catholics. As the Charismatic Renewal Movement spread across the country, a whole new kind of worship music evolved. Healings and deliverances were not unusual.

As Sukie began to sense that it was time for her to move beyond Billings, she enrolled in Asbury Theological Seminary in Kentucky. In preparation, she sold her house and furnishings and packed the rest of her belongings into her '71 red Ford Maverick coupe. The day before she was to leave, during prayer time, Sukie had a conversation with the Holy Spirit that went something like this:

H.S: "Where are you going?"

S: "I'm going to Kentucky to learn more   about You."

H.S: "I'd rather you went to Seattle."

S: "Why didn't you tell me before this last   minute?"

H.S: "You didn't ask me."

S: "OH!"

The next evening, after Sukie informed her prayer partners of her change in plans, they all gathered to pray for her before she left. One of the men in the group handed Sukie a note and said, "I'm so glad you are headed to Seattle. When you get there, call these people. They may be able to help you."

Sukie drove over the Rocky Mountains in the middle of winter, arrived safely in Seattle and called the folks named in the note. A friendly couple welcomed her to their home, where she stayed until she found a job and an apartment.

With all of Seattle to choose from, Sukie happened to find an apartment close to the Methodist church on Queen Anne Hill, in the area where my family lived. That Methodist church is where Sukie and I first met.

CHAPTER NINE

Importing Sukie from Tokyo

As told by Bill
Approved by Sukie

After a year in Seattle, Sukie decided that she needed to return to Tokyo. Her father had died, and her older sister had taken over the affairs of the family's elderly survivors. Her sister had developed a deep resentment of Sukie's becoming a Christian. Her sister was so angry that she somehow managed to have Sukie's name removed from government records.

When Sukie returned to Tokyo, she found a place to live, found a temp job with Manpower and cleaned up the mess with her citizenship records. She also got connected with a network of Christians who became her new "family."

In due course, Sukie got a very demanding job as special assistant to the head of Occidental Petroleum's operations in Tokyo. She had an American "green card" which authorized her to work in the U.S. To keep it current. she would come back to visit Seattle every summer. That's when I began to enter the picture.

Earlier in life, I had made a serious mistake that resulted in the collapse of my marriage. I had become super busy building an employee benefit consulting business, helping with a Boy Scout troop, and helping my pastor reach out to young folks caught up in the '60s drug scene, to name only a few of my distractions. All good stuff, it seemed at the time, but I failed to protect "my castle." One of the guys I thought I was helping by allowing him to live in my home, took a shine to my wife and literally captured her mentally, emotionally and physically. My marriage crashed and burned, and I ended up a single dad with three teenagers.

After a couple of years, when Sukie was visiting Seattle doing her green card thing, we decided to get acquainted by going through the book of Luke, passage by passage, making cassette tape recordings of our thoughts. We each had a high-tech Walkman cassette recorder and would record and exchange tapes regularly by mail.

When I would get a tape from Sukie, I'd play it every time I got in my car and I began to discover what was in her head and heart, and it was good. By the time we finished our commentaries on the book of Luke, I had fallen in love with Sukie's character and her voice!

When I managed to cobble together a trip to Japan, Sukie agreed to put me up at her place and introduce me to her mother. She picked me up at the airport in the red Maverick. In those days, it was a tank, compared to the early Hondas and Toyotas. Off we went into her world which included hunting for a different apartment, as the building she was living in was about to be demolished. I soon learned that this was no small feat, since to move, she not only needed to find an apartment, but the apartment also had to have a certified parking space for her car. After a couple of days of searching, I gathered enough courage to suggest to her that she forget about Tokyo and come back to Seattle and marry me. She said, "Why should I?" I said, "Because you need a place to park your car!"

It was the toughest sale I ever made, but eventually Sukie showed up in Seattle with all her worldly goods in two suitcases. And with a beautiful Japanese-bred poodle under her arm. She had gotten the poodle for her elderly mother, then discovered it was too much for her mom to handle.

It was August, and we had an outdoor wedding at the University of Washington arboretum. Sukie moved in with me and my three teenagers, Chris, Sara and Peter, and our snarly three-legged mutt who didn't take kindly to her poodle. "Heaven on earth," I said, and I can only imagine what Sukie was thinking.

Within two years, all three kids had moved out to pursue their own dreams. Sukie and I were alone at last. Getting our marriage together became our top priority, so we rented the house, moved into an apartment, unplugged the phone, and spent two years making four decisions.

- The first decision was to find a more balanced church community than the Methodist box we were in.
- The second decision was for me to stay in the business world and no longer entertain thoughts of going to Bible school to learn how to do the Lord's work.
- The third decision was to establish a home of our own.
- The fourth decision was to raise a family, an idea that had never occurred to me before we got married.

Here's an illustration of the intensity of our decision-making process. Sukie learned of an Assembly of God community that was very active and so we visited on a couple of Sundays. We made an appointment to get acquainted with the pastor, who invited us to visit the Wednesday evening prayer and praise service.

This church change was a big deal for me, because throughout my divorce and remarriage, my Methodist pastor had become a precious, faithful friend. In changing churches, I felt disloyal to my friend. Sukie and I had many discussions about it, but eventually we ran out of things to say. Regardless, Sukie was fully committed to our decision to change churches and I was fully committed to Sukie.

When Wednesday came around, Sukie and I had nothing more pressing to do, so we went to the service at the Assemblies of God church and slipped into the back row. The pastor spotted us and said, "We have new folks among us tonight and I want to introduce them to you. Bill and Sukie, please come up here so everyone can meet you." Sukie looked at me, wide-eyed.

We went forward and when we got to the front, the pastor, at 6'4"and 250 pounds, bent over and held the microphone in Sukie's direction. He asked her to tell everyone what the Lord was doing in her life. She looked up at him and said, "It's really hard to talk about how good the Lord is when you haven't spoken to your husband in three days!" Everyone broke out in laughter. We went home laughing and talking and moved on with our other decisions.

Remember, this all took place almost 40 years ago. Both of us had been baptized in the Holy Spirit and had received the gift of a prayer language. But we knew nothing about the other gifts of the Holy Spirit, nothing about the level of intimacy He desired to have with us, and especially nothing about the seemingly irreligious idea that He wanted to and could become our best friend!

We were praying to the Lord, but in our limited understanding, He was in Heaven, not living in our hearts with our Spirit. So, we just plowed on, living without consciously depending on His direct involvement. Some of the ground that we were about to plow was full of rocks!

CHAPTER TEN

Korean Adoptions

As told by Bill

Based on our decision to raise a family together, Sukie and I started exploring adoption. In the 1960s, post-war poverty in Korea was so severe that it created an opportunity for massive numbers of adoptions of Korean children by American citizens. We managed to qualify to adopt two girls.

Early in the adoption process, Sukie began to express concern about how her mother would respond to the girls, as her mother's generation in old Japan didn't get along with Koreans. Sukie came up with the idea of giving the little girls beautiful Japanese names—Youkie and Akarie. And it worked, Sukie's mother never knew the difference; our two new daughters were her Japanese granddaughters.

On the other hand, my own mother was having her own issues with the idea of first having a Japanese daughter-in-law and then having Korean grandkids, to boot. Sukie dealt with this dilemma. My folks were living in a large retirement home in Seattle. The retirement home had a formal dining room. Every so often, we would be invited to join them there for dinner; Sukie would dress the girls to the nines with bows in their hair, frilly dresses, white tights and black patent leather shoes. We would arrive at the last minute and the girls would hustle through the dining room to be with their grandparents. All the old ladies would "oooh" and "aaah" at this scene with Peggy Laney's adorable, well-behaved granddaughters, and Sukie won my mother's heart as she became so proud to be grandmother to these beautiful little girls.

The adoption process was different for each child. Youkie was delivered to us in a special receiving room at the SeaTac airport. The volunteer delivery woman had started her journey to Seoul, Korea, about four days earlier, picked up the child, gotten on a flight to Seattle and found us for the hand-off.

The child was a beautiful little Asian doll. However, as the volunteer "pickup angel" finished the transfer paperwork, she turned to Sukie and said. "God be with you. This child is angry at the world."

Two years later, the pickup arrangement for Akarie was a whole different story. Sukie and I had to take a long flight to Seoul to get her. We arrived in Seoul on a cold, gray winter's day and managed to find the equally drab Korean Child Services building. We were about to begin a 34-year adventure that we could never have imagined. It began as a tired, middle-aged woman with a child bound in a cloth and strapped on her back, came into the room where we were waiting. She untied the cloth and lay the child on her back on a table. Without a word or eye contact, she changed the child's diaper, picked her up and handed her to me.

Sukie thought it was strange that the woman avoided eye contact, as if she had something to hide. Years later, we learned what it was, but, suffice it to say, that would be a whole 'nother book!

In my arms, Akarie hardly moved, her face and arms just puffy flesh. As I looked at her, under my breath, I said, "Lord, I wonder if there are eyeballs behind these puffy slits?"

Sukie wrapped Akarie in the new blanket she had brought for the occasion. I signed the necessary paperwork, including the birth certificate that said she was two years old.

By the time we got home, we had discovered that this child was in extremely poor condition. She could only grunt and cry, she could not roll over or even hold her bottle, which we discovered had a formula in it that was basically white sugar water. We did discover, however, that there were beautiful eyes behind those puffy slits in her small face.

As soon as possible after we got home, Sukie made an appointment with a well-respected pediatrician. After the doctor finished her examination, she told Sukie that this child was severely mentally and physically disabled. Akarie needed to be fed a special formula and we were to bring her back for a checkup in two weeks.

Sukie was devastated. However, with her heritage and life experiences, she had developed a core belief that God doesn't make mistakes and that failure was not an option. She got started with the special formula and under the guidance of a physical therapist, who was part of our church family, she began spending hours each day moving Akarie's arms and legs, and trying to get the formula into her. Akarie was not digesting what was being almost force-fed to her and she was simply shrinking. Sukie got her back to the doctor who gave Akarie a shot and said that if her condition didn't improve in the next four days, she would have to be hospitalized.

On the Sunday evening following that doctor's appointment, Sukie and I had planned to get a babysitter and attend a city-wide prayer and praise service in a large movie and performing arts theater in downtown Seattle. The speaker for the event was Bob Mumford, at the time, a key national leader of the Charismatic Renewal Movement.

So she could stay with Akarie, Sukie had opted out of the opportunity to hear Mumford speak and I ended up going with a friend. We were seated almost in the middle of a packed house. The time of prayer and praise was glorious. Mumford took the podium and began to teach about the Holy Spirit. Well into his presentation, he abruptly stopped and said, "This is not my calling, but I believe there are folks in this theater who are in need of physical healing, and I am asking you to get out of your seats and stand up, so we can pray for you."

It was almost as if I had heard a voice in my head saying, loud and clear, "Stand Up!" The urge was so powerful, that I turned to my friend and said to him, "I don't need healing, but Akarie does." I stood up and stretched out my arms as though I were holding her and prayed, "Jesus, Akarie is not here, but there was a centurion who said, "You have the authority." At that moment, I felt a powerful charge go through my body and I knew she was healed. As soon as I got home and told Sukie what happened, I asked her to just feed Akarie whatever was in the house—milk, eggs, ice cream, peanut butter, whatever we have, just feed her. She did and it worked! The doctor was amazed and we were overjoyed. We didn't know it at the time, but it was the Holy Spirit doing the healing and it was a super slingshot.

Looking back on all those years, Sukie and I have come to believe that the Lord was using this renewal movement to break down the denominational walls of His Church through a massive introduction of the gifts of the Holy Spirit. The gift of a prayer language in worship and praise gatherings, in theaters like the one I was in that night, were common throughout the country.

About six months later, Sukie had another experience with one of those Holy Spirit slingshots. She had been spending hours upon hours trying to get a response out of Akarie, and even though her leg and arm muscles were beginning to tighten up, there was never a smile, just whines, whimpers and grunts. Suke lost her patience one afternoon, when she finished Akarie's physical therapy routine and was exhausted and frustrated to the max. She got down on her knees and yelled right into Akarie's face, "I hate you, you ugly demon, and I command you in the name of Jesus to get out of Akarie. Leave her alone and go back to hell!" There was no response. Exasperated, Sukie lay down on the nearby couch. Then, a few minutes later, she heard a cluck, cluck, cluck sound. She sat up and here was Akarie, standing up and leaning into the couch. She had picked up a toy and was looking at it with an impish grin on her face. When Sukie met me at the door that evening, her eyes were dancing with joy.

A few days later, Akarie began to speak in English and in full sentences. Who would believe all this, we wondered? A few years later when Sukie was studying for her masters in mental health and counseling, she learned that what we were dealing with was a child with multiple personalities. As we discovered, these personalities developed as a result of the abuse (especially sexual abuse) and abandonment that Akarie had experienced before we got her. We believe what happened that afternoon was that when the demon got thrown out, one of Akarie's numerous other personalities was free to take control, and that person was sharp as a tack and a delight to be with.

Our adventure in raising Akarie and her sister Youkie is too complicated to include in this book. Suffice it to say, we were surely imperfect parents. I kept telling Sukie, "Relax, they will be okay. After all, I've been through this before and all three of my kids turned out just fine." She would respond, "These are not the typical strong-willed kids that Dr James Dobson (an expert on the strong-willed child) writes about. These girls had an extremely tough start and their healing is going to be a long, hard journey." Sukie was right, but looking back, we realize it would all have been a lot less stressful had we only known and recognized that Holy Spirit was right there with us, and anxious to guide us day by day through it all, had we just invited Him.

CHAPTER ELEVEN

How Sukie and I Got from Seattle

To Bradenton

As told by Bill

Moving to Bradenton has played the most significant part in the journey of faith that Sukie and I have experienced. I am truly convinced today that we were led here by the Holy Spirit and that our story is an excellent example of how Holy Spirit will not only speak to us directly but also through the words and actions of those around us.

It was late December 1999; Sukie and I were experiencing great stress in our marriage. Whatever triggered the meltdown, it was serious enough that she was living in the upstairs part of our home, I was living in the basement, and we weren't talking about anything but the lousy weather. At that point we had been married for 17 years, living in Seattle and were now empty nesters. Youkie and Akarie were adults, out of the house and charting their own courses.

It was a week before Christmas, when I said to Sukie something to the effect of, "You know, Honey, Christmas is coming. We're not talking or living together and if we hang around Seattle making nice, we will be the biggest hypocrites in town. Let's just get out of here. I know a guy who has a condo in Mexico. Maybe it would be available." "No Way," she said, and walked away.

The next day, I noticed Sukie was working on her computer and, sure enough, she had found a cancellation for a three-week stay in a one-bedroom condo on the beach in a place called Anna Maria Island on the west coast of Florida. She had booked it and we were leaving in three days.

Later, she told me that the "No Way" response had to do with going with me to some remote place in Mexico, where she couldn't easily escape if things went sour.

I was scheduled to spend the next day helping John Kruger, my closest friend and an associate in a little non-profit called International Fellowship. For about 20 years as part of International Fellowship, John and his wife, Jean, had been doing the Lord's work in Kenya and Eastern Europe. They were on R & R in Seattle and he was spending the day putting cedar shingles on his son's garage on Bainbridge Island. I grabbed some tools, caught the ferry, and joined him in shingling the garage.

While banging away, I told John about the Florida Christmas trip, and that I was going to take along a few faith-based living books I had been reading, for Sukie. "You're going to do what?" he shouted. "Damn it, Bill, forget the books; just listen to her!" How's that for great Christian counseling?

On the way back to Seattle on the ferry, I got one of those messages in my head, "Call George Smith." George was a friend who owned a jewelry shop. I had never given Sukie a real diamond engagement ring. When we got married, I was so broke that all she got was a wedding band. Years later, I gave her a ring with a zirconia stone, not the real thing.

As there were no cell phones in those days, I called George when I got home. "I need to borrow a diamond ring for about three weeks. When I return, if I can't use it, I'll give it back to you. But if Sukie keeps it, I'll sell the house and pay you for it." "Fair enough," he said. "I think I know Sukie's ring size and I'm sure there's a diamond in the safe that would do the job. Come down to the shop tonight at nine and I'll fix you up." Later that night I left his shop with a diamond ring in a little white box in my pocket. It had been quite a day.

Two days later, Sukie and I were in Bradenton, driving west on Manatee Avenue to the Inn on the Beach on Anna Maria Island. It was nextdoor to the all-you-can-eat pancake breakfast stand on the beach. We moved in. Sukie got the bedroom and I got the sleeper couch in the living room. The next day was Christmas. I set the white box on the coffee table. She picked it up. "What's this?" she asked. I said, "It's the real thing, that's been a long time coming." She opened it and said, "It's nice" and put the ring back in the box.

That morning, Sukie began to talk and I began to really listen. She had a memory like a computer hard drive that included virtually every event since we first met. She was not angry or bitter or disappointed, just exhausted, and needed to empty her heart. For me, it was like having a root canal–every day!

Much of our journey together had been fantastic, from my perspective. But I didn't remember much of what she was recounting. And the events I did remember, I had often ignored or I hadn't paid attention to how she was internalizing what was going on.

Every morning, I retreated to that magnificent Anna Maria beach to clear my head and thank the Lord for where we were and what was happening. The warmth of that big yellow ball in the sky while we were exploring the island, was beginning to thaw Sukie out. In Seattle she was cold most of the time.

she would put on her frilly long underwear in October and not take it off till July. Peace was beginning to settle our souls.

About the eighth morning on the beach, I heard a very clear voice in my head say, "Move here!" What? Me move from Seattle to Florida and leave behind my family, my business, my place in the body of Christ, my home, my lifetime of relationships, abandon all my ego-stroking life in Seattle?

When this one-sided discussion was over, I turned around, hiked back to the inn and said to Sukie, "Let's move here. I'll semi-retire and commute every two weeks. We can make it work."

Astonished, Sukie looked at me and said, "Would you really do that?" I said "Yes." That night she climbed into bed with me with the ring on.

And that is how we got to Bradenton. And now we've been here for more than 20 years and we can't adequately express our thankfulness to the Lord for the wonderful results of those Holy Spirit slingshots.

CHAPTER TWELVE

Speaking in Tongues

As told by Bill

This story begins in 1959. Dennis Bennett was the rector of the 2000-member St. Marks Episcopal Church in Van Nuys, California. Evidently, it was successful pastoring as usual for Father Bennett, until one day a young couple came into his office and told him about an experience they had while being baptized in the Holy Spirit and receiving the gift of tongues as a prayer language.

As Bennett describes it in his book, *Nine O'clock In the Morning,* his curiosity was aroused. After some weeks of research in his Bible and attending a small group that gathered around this couple, Bennett, himself, received the precious gift of a prayer language, and he began to share it with his flock. In due course, conflicts began to develop among the receivers and non-receivers and Bennett resigned to prevent the parish from braking apart.

The Episcopal Bishop for Western Washington heard about the "happening" in Van Nuys (even Newsweek and Time magazines had featured articles about the Episcopalians speaking in tongues) and he offered the unemployed Bennett a post at St. Luke's Episcopal Church, a small, dying parish in Ballard, an old neighborhood in Seattle.

As he tells the story in his book, Bennett spent the first weeks at his new post getting acquainted with the old-timers who had been doing their best to keep the doors of their small church open. Then, one of the couples asked him if he would be willing to come to a Friday evening gathering in their home so they could hear his story about what happened in Van Nuys. That gathering rolled over to the next Friday evening, and to the next, until the Holy Spirit showed up and the entire gathering began to joyously speak in unknown prayer languages.

Months later, there was such new life in the little Episcopal church that it was decided to open the doors every Friday night and invite the curious public to come and hear Father Bennett and his enthusiastic parishioners share their stories.

Eight years earlier, I had left Seattle to attend the University of Michigan. When I returned, I had a wife, named Patty, two kids, a business degree, two years' active duty as an Air Force officer and an emerging curiosity about Jesus.

Patty and I settled down, bought a house and had a third child. I went to work with my dad and his partner in the insurance business. Because it was the "appropriate" thing for us to do, we also started attending the downtown Seattle First Methodist Church, where my folks had been members for many years. After a few months of warming "the Laney pew" in the balcony of that old church, we bailed out and transferred to a seemingly more active neighborhood Methodist church with Sunday school for the children and Wednesday evening potluck dinners.

During all those years of Sunday school and sermons and repeating the words of the Apostles Creed about Father, Son and Holy Ghost, I didn't have a clue about the role of the Holy Spirit in my life. So, when we heard about a "Holy Spirit happening" in a little Episcopal church in Ballard, and there were meetings for the curious public every Friday evening, Patty and I decided to have a Friday date night and go see what it was all about.

Patty and I knew nothing of the Van Nuys backstory, but sure enough, the night we showed up, there was Father Bennett in his casual priestly garb. He quietly reviewed references to the Holy Spirit in the Books of Acts and John, and told his story about receiving the gift of tongues.

At the end of his presentation, Father Bennett invited anyone who wanted to receive the gift of a private prayer language to come to the altar. The way he revealed the nature of the Holy Spirit in the scriptures and told his story made so much sense to me that I decided to go forward. There, on my knees at that Episcopal communion rail, I began to babble in a language that I never heard before!

Over the next few months I discovered that this language was with me all the time and I was thoroughly enjoying singing and worshiping the Lord with it. Then, one day when I was driving my VW Bug and listening to the King's Garden Christian radio station, I caught a special announcement from the Methodist bishop, admonishing his fellow Methodists to stay away from the inappropriate teachings that were coming from St. Luke's Epicopal Church in Ballard. Now, I may not be the brightest guy on the planet, but the Air Force had taught me something about command and control. Here was my "spiritual commander" telling me to stay away from St. Luke's and I'd already been there! So, I simply quit using my new prayer language, and it was gone.

For the next two to three years my journey turned into a deeper love affair with Jesus in many other wonderful ways. Accepting an invitation to attend a weekend conference in Calgary, Canada, with a bunch of Canadian Christian guys, I somehow managed to get to the gathering and found myself immersed in the pool-of-love-and-joy-in-the-Lord that those guys welcomed me into.

On Saturday night when I got back to my hotel room, I got down on my knees beside the bed and said to the Lord, "I'm so full of Your love and peace that I would sure like to get that speaking in tongues gift back, so I could worship you more completely than I can with just my language." I stayed there until my knees began to hurt. Nothing happened.

Dejected, I climbed into bed and called it a day. When the gathering ended on Sunday, I headed home, routed through the Vancouver airport. While passing through the customs checkpoint, I looked across to an adjoining line and there was Father Bennett, clerical collar and all under his overcoat. "Isn't this amazing," I thought!

As we emerged into the open space in the terminal I caught up with him and said, "Hey, Father Bennett, you don't know who I am but I know who you are." Then, as we walked toward our connecting flights, I told him the story of what had happened to me since that night, kneeling at St. Luke's alter, as he facilitated my receiving the gift of a prayer language.

"That gift is yours forever"

With a grin he responded, "No problem. That gift is yours forever. It's still there. All you need to do is find a quiet place, invite His presence, open your mouth and let sound come out and it will be there." We split toward different gates. The whole encounter lasted about ten minutes.

What kind of answer to prayer is that?

Later that evening, alone in my car, sitting in the rain in the remote SeaTac parking lot, I grabbed the steering wheel, followed instructions and began to sing. Bingo, there it was.

This wonderful prayer language has been bubbling up as pure joy from my inner being ever since. What an incredible gift. And what a unique physical reminder that the third spiritual person of the Trinity is actually in residence in my body!"

I now realize that speaking in tongues as a prayer language is one of the nine gifts that Paul names as part of the Baptism of the Holy Spirit. However, it appears to me that this is the only one of the gifts that is ours to keep and use for the rest of our lives. And, who knows, maybe forever. Evidently, the rest of the gifts are parceled out to a receptive believer from time to time at the Holy Spirit's discretion. For example, if in exercising the gift of healing, you prayed for a disabled person who then experienced miraculous healing, it wouldn't mean that you own the gift of healing.

I have also come to realize that the Holy Spirit enters into every person who makes the decision that Jesus is their personal Savior. The rest of the life of that person then becomes a journey of learning to recognize and access the gifts that come with that decision.

As I look back over the 50 years since I first encountered the Holy Spirit and received the gift of a prayer language, it appears to me that what I got was akin to dessert before dinner.

The main course of friendship with a spiritual being named Holy Spirit wasn't served until my wife Sukie and I were given an opportunity to facilitate a Bayside Community Church small group. We studied Robert Morris's book *The God I Never Knew*. Now, at age 87, I can wholeheartedly declare that Holy Spirit has indeed became my best friend and that's the main course!

As Sukie recently observed, "Looking back, it seems as though the real results of the Holy Spirit Charismatic Renewal in the '70s and 80s' was the beginning of dissolution of the denominational separations that infected the body of Christ. We were so busy loving one another and excited to be worshiping together, that our old differences just melted away."

However, I think the renewal simply ran out of steam because it was taking place primarily outside of the traditional churches. It was focused almost entirely on contemporary worship music and speaking in tongues and lacked the in-depth teaching we are now receiving about all of the gifts of the Holy Spirit.

In Romans 5:5 of the Message Bible, Eugene Peterson restates Paul's writings as this wonderful thought: "We can't round up enough containers to hold everything God graciously pours into our lives through the Holy Spirit."

CHAPTER THIRTEEN

Selected Short Stories

As told by Bill & Andy

The Greatest Gift My Dad Ever Gave to Me

As told by Bill

My dad was a good Methodist and a self-employed life insurance salesman. In the mid-1920s he made enough money to feed his family, pay the electric bill and make a down payment on a house on Queen Anne Hill in Seattle. When the Depression hit, he was unable to make the house payments, so he gave it back to the bank. But the bank couldn't sell it for the amount of the mortgage, so the bank rented it back to my folks at half the mortgage payment. Three years later, income began to improve, and my folks bought the house back from the bank.

After the World War II, Dad partnered with a younger man and formed an insurance brokerage firm. They had a buy and sell agreement which required Dad to retire at age 65. When I returned from the Air Force and settled in Seattle, I had the opportunity to work with the firm during Dad's last year there before retiring. His partner was my boss. My job was selling group medical insurance to small companies and I went after the assignment with considerable vigor.

One afternoon after observing my approach to people for a couple of months, my dad invited me out to coffee and shared this wisdom with me. "I've been observing your work son and wondered if you would be up for a suggestion?" I said, "Sure." After all, he was paying for the coffee.

Dad: "Tell me, son, in the English language how is a strong statement punctuated?"

Bill: "With an exclamation point."

Dad: "Right, now if you took that exclamation mark and made it three-dimensional and blew it up to three feet, what would it look like?"

Bill: "Maybe a baseball bat,"

Dad: "Right, and if someone is swinging a baseball bat at you, how would you react?"

Bill: "I'd probably pull back, put up my arms in defense and get out of there."

Dad: "Oh, so you wouldn't be attracted to that person or the message he or she was trying to give to you?"

Bill: "No, I'd have a tough time listening. Come to think of it, I would probably have the same reaction to a person who simply talked at me about whatever was on his or her mind".

Dad: "Now, Son, tell me, how is a sentence with a question punctuated?"

Bill: "With a question mark."

Dad: "Ok, you're two for two. So again, visualize making that question mark three dimensional and stretching it out to maybe six feet and tell me what that might remind you of?"

Bill: "Even though I've never held one, it might be a shepherd's staff."

Dad: "Right again, and how did the shepherds use the staff?"

Bill: "I suppose to reach out and pull a wandering sheep back into the herd."

Dad: "Right again. Now how do you respond to a gently asked question?"

Bill "Oh Dad, I get it. That's what *you* do all the time and everybody responds well to you".

From that day forward, I made it my purpose to emulate my dad and include as many questions as possible in every conversation. It's the most valuable gift he ever gave me. And to top it all off, he paid for the coffee.

Holy Spirit to the Rescue
Carey's Story

As told by Andy

This happened quite recently. My wife Marsha felt an urge to pray for one of our daughters. Carey was training for a management position in a national grocery/drugstore chain. At first, Marsha felt she should pray because Carey was asked to create a powerpoint training presentation to encourage employees to show customers how to approve text updates for prescription refills. As Marsha was praying, she felt prompted to go deeper in prayer for Carey and her family, which she did. She also texted Carey, "I'm Praying for you."

At that very moment, two unfamiliar men who appeared to be high on drugs came into Carey's store. One went back to the pharmacy, the other went straight to the hardware section and grabbed some packages of Xacto razor knives. The pharmacist had the physique of a linebacker. Whatever the man who went back there had planned, he changed his mind and headed back toward the cashier.

Carey felt the cashier might be in trouble and went to the front of the store. She saw the second man trying to put socks on his hands. Carey asked him, "Are you planning to rob the store?" The cashier reached for the store phone and dialed 911. The other man with the razor knife packages was unsuccessfully trying to open one. The cashier said, "I'm on the phone with the police right now." Both men ran out of the store.

At that very moment, an off-duty sheriff's deputy walked in and the cashier yelled, "They tried to rob us!" The deputy chased the men next door as three police cars showed up. Later, the deputy returned to the store to get the energy drink she had come to purchase. She said she normally shopped at one of the other stores closer to her home, but on that day decided to try this particular store.

It seems as though Holy Spirit often guides people to take exactly the right actions such as a sheriff's deputy coming into a store at that precise moment in response to the prayers of a believer. There are many who would call this all coincidence, but Marsha and I believe that there are no coincidences with God. There are Holy Spirit slingshots— deadly accurate and right on time. We are ever so grateful for this one.

Holy Spirit In a Jail Cell
Jonathan's Story

As told by Andy

One of the best things Bayside Community Church offers is a growth track. One of the growth track programs is called, "My Freedom." It is designed as an encouragement for participants to   communicate with God and walk in the freedom that comes from it.

From time to time, Marsha and I have had the privilege of facilitating My Freedom; a seven-week study that includes participation in a small group to discuss daily readings that include the Holy Spirit and what He is doing in our lives. Often, we feel we receive more blessings from facilitating the group than we did when we first went through the study ourselves. We go through the study again each time we lead a group, and feel that Holy Spirit just takes us deeper each time.

If you have ever wondered if there was a prescribed formula for receiving a private prayer language from the Holy Spirit, let this next example set your heart at ease.

In one of the groups we led, we met a young man Jonathan. He was a relatively new believer but seemed to have quite a bit of knowledge of the Bible and what it says about the Holy Spirit. Once he got comfortable with the group, Jonathan shared that he had spent time in prison. During his incarceration, he started reading the Bible. As he described it, he had a lot of time to read, so he read the Bible several times.

As Jonathan read the bible, he would often pray. In one particular prison prayer session, he realized he was speaking in a language he did not recognize. After what felt like five minutes, he became aware of the time. His prayer had lasted nearly an hour. This was Jonathan's introduction to the Holy Spirit.

Lunch with Eugene Peterson
Author of The Message Bible
As told by Bill

During the years when I was commuting from Bradenton to Seattle every two weeks, I was hanging out at the condo of our friends' John and Jean Kruger while they were in Kenya. One morning, I got a call from a lady friend. "Hey, Bill, Eugene Peterson is in town on a book tour. He finally finished adding the Old Testament to *The Message* Bible and is speaking at a luncheon today at the Mercer Island Presbyterian Church. I have an extra ticket. Do you want to go?"

"DO I EVER!" I had read much of what Peterson had written over the years and he was my all-time favorite Christian Author.

When I climbed into my friend's car, I said, "If I get to meet this guy, I am going to ask him, how he got the time and discipline to do this incredible job?" She replied, "Good luck."

When we arrived at the church, we were guided to the large gym behind the sanctuary and to the buffet line. As I came out of the line with my friend, a hostess pointed us to a couple of empty seats at a nearby round table. My friend took the closest seat and I went over and set my tray next to hers. The man in the next seat was dressed all in black: shirt, jeans and cowboy boots. I stuck out my hand and said "Hi, I'm Bill Laney." He took my hand and said, "Hi, I'm Eugene Peterson."

After chit-chat around the table subsided, I asked him, "How did you ever manage to get the time and discipline to do this job?" He said, "If you really want to know, I'll tell you." The table went quiet and he started. "Both my folks had died and my wife and I inherited the family cabin on Big Lake in Montana. I took a six-month sabbatical from teaching at Regent College near Vancouver. We winterized the cabin and moved in. I set up an office in one of the bedrooms and went to work four to five hours a day."

I asked, "What did you do? Did you start with the King James Bible, or the New American Standard?"

"Oh no, no," he said "Every day I picked up where I left off the day before. I read it in Greek, I read it in Hebrew. Then I went back and re-wrote it in language familiar to teenagers and young adults."

The meeting started, and Eugene Peterson gave a short talk. I bought an autographed copy of his new complete *Message Bible* and used it regularly until it showed up in a more convenient size on the phone in my pocket.

As I look back, I can now explain the remarkable occurrence of my meeting and conversing with Eugene Peterson as another one of those divine Holy Spirit slingshots.

Profound Truths Learned 50 Years Ago

As told by Bill

The first time I ever heard from God with what seemed like a clear, spoken word in my head was in Marrakesh, a place I never expected to see. Marrakesh is a centuries old trading town in the center of Morocco in northwest Africa.

This is the backstory on why I was in Marrakesh. About six months after my first marriage failed, I was not functioning well at the office. My partners finally confronted me with their prescription for getting my head back on track: "Take a month off and get out of town."

That advice set up a chain of events that turned out to be one of the most incredible healing and bonding experiences I could ever imagine. Chris, my 17-year-old son, was spending that winter in the French Alps working as an au pair (mother's helper) for a family with four boys under age five. In addition to his work, and skiing and having a great time, he was also learning French so he could graduate from high school; he needed a foreign language credit.

Chris found an old VW bus for sale for $800. It was a classic hippy outfitted rectangular box. It was at least ten years old but still running great. It even had a portable bunk set up with four air mattresses plus a full-size roof rack for our ski gear. A couple in our church heard about our opportunity and offered to chip in $400 for the bus if, at the end of our trip, we would leave it for them at the Frankfurt airport. So, I pulled Peter, 15, and Sara, 13, out of school, and we met Chris in Chamonix, France. We skied for a couple of days, then piled into the bus and hit the road, headed south with no schedule except to get the bus to Frankfurt in three weeks.

On our journey, we visited the memorial site of Dachau, a German concentration camp where untold thousands of Jews and others died horrible deaths during World War II. At the end of the tour we came across a large, dome-shaped structure with a wide brick path leading into an underground room. In the open space there was a small, roped off area where visitors could meet and chat with whoever was sitting there on a stool. To our benefit, the stool was occupied by an elderly Lutheran priest who was a survivor of the unspeakable torture of having been imprisoned in this camp. This was now his volunteer post for a few hours every day. When it was my turn to approach him, I asked, "Tell me sir, how do you explain all this?". His simple profound answer was, *"The evil one was loosed without fetter."*

We worked our way through Switzerland, around through Yugoslavia, then down to Greece. From there we caught an overnight ferry around Italy to the southern coast of France. From there, we drove to Gibraltar where we caught another ferry across the Strait of Gibraltar to Tangier, and from there to Marrakesh.

With this compressed tour description, you can imagine that we were having the time of our lives; healing, bonding, meeting people and learning about that part of the world. Peter, Chris and I had only one complaint. About every three days, Sara would look for a place where we could spend the night so she could wash her hair.

During this time, I had a running discussion with God. In the early mornings as I was reading the Living Bible, in John 14:6 I came across this: Jesus said, "I am the way, the truth, and the life. No one can come to the Father except through me." I thought that this was the most pompous, discriminatory, exclusive criterion I could imagine, and, what about all the people who never got to know Jesus?

Here we were in the very heart of the Muslim world which I knew absolutely nothing about. The women were draped head to toe in black burkas with only their eyes exposed. Wen we passed them, some Passing by, some would look away, others would make eye contact with their big, beautiful black eyes.

Most of the men wore a white wraparound outfit and carried a portable knee pad for kneeling because five times a day the automatic speaker system hanging on the minaret towers of the local mosques would blast out a call to prayer. Everything would stop and the men would fall to their knees wherever they were to pray. When we got home, I looked it up and learned that in the proper position for kneeling prayer, only five parts of the body are to touch the ground—toes, knees, hands, nose and forehead.

On the afternoon of our last dayin Marrakesh, while the kids had returned to the huge open air market to trade their American clothes for whatever they could get, I went for a jog. I found myself outside the walls of the town, in front of an ancient mud-plastered mosque. The mosque that I was staring at had an arched, wooden door with a scroll above it that read, "Europeans Not Welcome."

I was alone but somehow aware of the Lord's presence. I said to Him, "What is all this? What am I looking at?" He responded, *"It's a counterfeit—they've all been siphoned off."*

I never again questioned John 14:6.

Sara and I needed to get home ASAP so we decided we would fly home and Chris and Peter would take the VW bus to the Frankfurt airport for our friends to pick up. Early the next morning, we started home. We caught the ferry back to Gibraltar and headed to the nearest international airport which was in Portugal. At the airport, I gave the boys their return tickets to Seattle and all the currency and coin we had left over from our $30 daily allowance. We prayed for blessings over them and sent them on their way. About ten days later, the phone rang at dinner time, "Hey Dad, Peter and I are at SeaTac. I bummed a quarter to call you. How about picking us up?"

Now I ask you—how's that for good seat-of-the pants parenting?

CHAPTER 14

A Final Thought to Ponder

Written by Pastor Rick Cusack
Bayside Community Church – West Bradenton Campus

During a recent lunch, I said to my dear friend Bill, "Would you like to hear a Holy Spirit story about your friend Evy?"
As always, Bill was anxious to hear about the Holy Spirit moving in my life and he leaned in. I began telling him about how Evy's story was brought to our Campus Pastor Mark Childers and how he called me into his office to tell me about it. Mark told me that a transgender, a member of our church, had trasnitoned to a man.

After many years of silence, she heard again from Holy Spirit who said that she was to transition back and she obeyed. Pastor Mark told me that this was very unusual as almost all transgenders do not transition back (detransition) and that it was a big deal. There was going to be a celebration here at our church and friends of Evy's would be attending, some flying in from out-of-town to be a part of this. He shared with me that he had been asked to pray for Evy with the group and to lead the celebration. Mark said, "I am going to be out of town for that weekend, so I need you to take my place and lead the prayer for Evy." "Well of course," I said. "That's what we do here, right? We pray for people."

On that Sunday, I remember coming to the church and as I made my way around to meet and greet many of our guests, I noticed a grouping of folks and I saw Bill and knew that was Evy's group. Introductions were made and the group moved into the auditorium. As the service began, I found myself not really paying attention to the message, but just wandering in my thoughts, until my eye caught Evy just a few rows in front of me.

As I sat there looking at her, Holy Spirit began to speak to me. He said, "You know, you are no different from Evy." To be honest, this caught me off guard, so I paused, in disagreement, because I didn't feel that I was similar at all to Evy, in that I was not transgender. But the Holy Spirit spoke again to me in that quiet, peaceful and loving voice. He said, "Yes, you are exactly the same as she."

As I paused again, just about to disagree, Holy Spirit said, "You have been trying your entire life to be someone I did not create you to be." Wow! As I began to let that set in, Holy Spirit went on to say, "There is no condemnation and there is no shame in what she has done. Today is a day of celebration, for she truly realizes her identity as a godly woman."

As the service ended, I approached the group and I remember asking Evy how she wanted me to pray for her. She told me she wanted to share her testimony, to tell her story. I remember telling her to look around, "It's already happening. Your story is being told and we are so proud of you." I prayed a prayer that day. I do not remember what I said, but I do know that the Holy Spirit moved in a mighty way through me and we celebrated our dear friend Evy.

Each and every weekend I look forward to seeing Evy in the church lobby and I always give her a hug and a smile. I'll never forget her, because it was through her that not only her story was told, but I realized that I too could truly become *who God created me to be.*

Author's Note

We hope you have found joy and inspiration in the stories we have shared. We also hope that within your own circle of influence, you will talk and hear about similar experiences. We have created a blog for people who wish to share their Holy Spirit slingshots for others to read and enjoy. You can find this blog at www.HolySpiritSlinsgshot.com

Finally, we pray God's blessing over each and every one of our readers and pray that they will come to know Holy Spirit and experience His power, love and friendship.

Holy Spirit References

A Micro Synopsis of the Holy Spirit's Presence on the Earth as found in various interpretations and translations of the Bible.

The Holy Spirit arrived on the scene very early in the creation story, "In the beginning God created the heavens and the earth. The earth was formless and empty, and darkness covered the deep waters. And the Spirit of God was hovering over the surface of the waters." (Genesis 1:1&2 NLT)

And God said, "Let **us** make mankind in **our** image, in our likeness..." (Genesis 1:26 NLT)

Then, long before Jesus showed up, the prophet Joel had this to say, "...I will pour out my Spirit on every kind of people: Your sons will prophesy, also your daughters. Your old men will dream, your young men shall see visions. I'll even pour out my Spirit on the who servants, men and women both."
(Joel 2:28 Msg)

Isaiah added this promise from the Lord... "For I will pour water on the thirsty land, and streams on dry ground. I will pour out my Spirit on your offspring and my blessing on your descendants." (Isaiah 44:3 NLT)

Many years later, the promised Spirit showed up and impregnated Mary. The angel answered, "The Holy Spirit will come on you, and the power of the Most High will overshadow you. So the Holy One to be born will be called the Son of God." (Luke 1:35 Msg)

Some 30 years later the Spirit appeared again when Jesus was being baptized by John... "and the Holy Spirit, in bodily form, descended on him like a dove. And a voice from heaven said, "You are my dearly loved Son, and you bring me great joy." (Luke 3:22 NLT)

Then Jesus began to teach his followers about his companion named Holy Spirit... "If you love me, show it by doing what I've told you. I will talk to the Father, and he will provide you another friend so you will always have someone with you. This friend is the Spirit of Truth. The Godless world can't take him in because it doesn't have eyes to see him, doesn't know what to look for. But you know him already because he has been staying with you, and will even be in you" (John 14:15-17 Msg)

"Anyone who believes in me may come and drink! For the Scriptures declare, 'Rivers of living waters shall flow from his heart'. When he said living waters he was speaking of the **Spirit** who would be given to everyone believing in him. But the **Spirit** had not yet been given, because Jesus had not yet entered into his glory." (John 7:37 Msg)

" Don't bargain with God. Be direct. Ask for what you need. This is not a cat-and-mouse, hide-and-seek game we're in. If your little boy asks for a serving of fish, do you scare him with a live snake on his plate? If your little girl asks for an egg, do you trick her with a spider? As bad as you are, you wouldn't think of such a thing—you're at least decent to your own children. And don't you think the Father who conceived you in love will give the Holy Spirit when you ask him? (Luke 11:10-13 Msg)

"Nevertheless I tell you the truth, it is to your advantage that I go away; for if I do not go away, the Helper will not come to you; but if I depart, I will send him to you... When He, the Spirit of Truth has come, He will guide you into all truth". (John 16:7&14 NLT)

Just before Jesus left the earth and moved back to heaven to be with His Father, he gave His disciples these instructions: "wait for what the Father promised: the promise you heard from me. John baptized in water; you will be baptized in the Holy Spirit. And soon." (Acts 1:4 Msg)

And then, forty days later:
"When the Feast of Pentecost came, they were all together in one place. Without warning there was a sound like a strong wind, gale force - no one could tell where it came from. It filled the whole building. Then, like a wildfire, the Holy Spirit spread through their ranks, and they started speaking in a number of different languages as the Spirit prompted them." (Acts 2: 1-4 Msg)

A few years later, Paul arrived on the scene and taught extensively about Holy Spirit, his wonderful friend and constant companion.

"All kinds of things are handed out by the Spirit, and to all kinds of people. The variety is wonderful:

- Wise counsel
- Clear understanding
- Simple trust
- Healing the sick
- Miraculous provision
- Proclamation
- Distinguishing between spirits
- Tongues
- Interpretation of tongues

All these gifts have a common origin, but are handed out one by one by the Spirit of God. He decides who gets what and when." 1 Corinthians 12:8-11 (Msg)

"I am grateful to God for the gift of praying in tongues that he gives us for praising him, which leads to wonderful intimacies we enjoy with him". (1 Corinthians 14:18-19 Msg)

And then, in the Message, Eugene Peterson, reinterprets Romans 8: 5 with this wonderful thought: "We cannot roundup enough containers to hold everything God generously pours into our lives thru the Holy Spirit".

And now, all these years later, Holy Spirit is gently knocking at your door offering you the most intimate relationship of all time!

Remember: Holy Spirit is God, as in Father, Son & Holy Spirit. They created you and everything needed to support you - and they love you!

Q & A about Naltrexone & the Sinclair Method

Most of the information we share about Naltrexone and alcoholism is available in Roy Eskapa's book, *The Cure for Alcoholism*. Anyone who is experiencing trouble with Alcohol would benefit from reading this definitive work.

Taking any medication comes with risk of side effects that must be discussed with your physician. In addition, be sure to do some of your own research on this and any other course of action you might take.

Q. What is Naltrexone?
A. According to Wikipedia, Naltrexone is an opioid antagonist that works by blocking the effects of opioids in the brain.

Q. What are Opioids?
A. Opioids are natural and synthetic drugs such as morphine, heroin, cocaine, oxycodone, and alcohol, that attach to opioid receptors in the brain.

Q. What is an antagonist?
A. In this context, an antagonist is a blocking agent.

Q. How can I obtain Naltrexone?
A. The most common form is a 50mg capsule available by prescription at most pharmacies.

Q. What does a month's supply cost without insurance?
A. In the big chain pharmacies in Bradenton Florida, 30 capsules cost between $109 and $120. However, the lowest price appears to be $39.07, purchased at participating pharmacies through

Q. What is The Sinclair Method (TSM) for healing Alcohol Use Disorder? (AUD is the scientific name for alcoholism).

A. Dr. David Sinclair was an American research scientist who spent his life searching for a way to cure alcoholism. He is credited with the discovery that taking one 50mg capsule of Naltrexone an hour before consuming alcohol would block the desire for more than one drink. Within 3-6 months, this routine extinguishes the desire for alcohol completely. The Sinclair Method web site (**www.the-sinclair-method.com/**) reports that TSM is 78 percent effective. We encourage you to review this site along with many other sites that come up when you google Naltrexone and The Sinclair Method.

Q. Is there a definitive book published about The Sinclair Method?
A. Yes. Roy Eskapa, PhD, wrote *The Cure for Alcoholism, the Medically Proven Way to Eliminate Alcohol Addiction*, published in 2008, and updated in 2012. This 337 page documentary paperback is currently available online and at bookstores.

Q. How much and for how long has Naltrexone been studied as a possible cure for AUD?

A. As reviewed in Eskapa's book, *The Cure For Alcoholism*, the first clinical trial was in 1978. Over the next 30 years, there were 113 published trials and research documents culminating with the 1,383 participant Project COMBINE, reviewed in the May 3ed, 2008, issue of the AMA Journal.

Q. When was Naltrexone approved by the FDA?

A. October, 2010.

Q. What should I do if my craving for alcohol has not disappeared after six months of faithfully taking one 50mg capsule of Naltrexone an hour before consuming any form of alcohol?

A. As recommended in the *The Cure for Alcoholism*, you should seek help from your doctor about increasing the dose of the Naltrexone capsule you are taking.

Q. Does "sweet preference" have anything to do with inhibiting the effectiveness of The Sinclair Method?

A. Some studies indicate that a person will be less likely to have the desired results of taking Naltrexone if, in additional to consuming alcohol, they are prone to consume large amount of sweet food and drink.

Q. Is TSM a form of gradual detoxification?

A. Yes. You start treatment with a physiological dependence on alcohol, but after several months of gradually reducing your drinking, you are consuming so little that you have your body has become detoxified.

Q. If on any day I'm not going to be drinking, should I take a capsule of Naltrexone anyway?
A. No. The pill without alcohol is as effective as a Tums for a headache. As strange as it may seem, the formula is: Naltrexone + Alcohol = the Cure.

Q. What planning is needed to stay on course indefinitely?
A. You need to develop a new habit of always having a pill available in your purse, your wallet or a pouch on your keychain, or in some other place that works for you.

Q. Is Naltrexone used in the treatment of addictions to opiates such as cocaine and heroin and synthetics like Oxycodone?
A. No. Treating opiate addictions is far more complex than treating AUD with The Sinclair Method. There is, however, an injectable form of Naltrexone that is used by many practionors in the field of drug addiction medication.

Q. Is The Sinclair Method an effective tool for social drinkers who want to reduce their alcohol consumption before they become alcoholics?
A. Yes.

Q. What are the most common medical conditions that would cause a person not to be a candidate for TSM?
A. Those with acute hepatitis or liver failure.

Q. Can Naltrexone be abused?
A. No. You cannot get high on it and it poses no addictive risks.

Q. Why isn't prescribing Naltrexone coupled with The Sinclair Method a well-known and widely applied treatment for AUD?   A. The counterintuitive nature of prescribing a pill to take with consuming alcohol may be difficult for some doctors to overcome. Also, at this point, there may be little profit incentive for a pharmaceutical company to produce and promote this generic drug. In addition, the lack of commercial promotion for this inexpensive, do-it-yourself-TSM-cure may have something to do with its disruptive threat to the profitable abstinence based programs and facilities industry.

Q. How do I Know when I'm Cured?
A. As spelled out in *The Cure for Alcoholism*, here are the main indicators of success:
- You are drinking less or not drinking at all.
- You're craving levels are way down or non-existent.
- Your mood has improved and you feel better physically and emotionally.
- Hangovers are history.
- Others notice that you are drinking less.
- Alcohol no longer dominates your thoughts or rules your life, and you have stopped obsessing about the next drink.
- You have simply lost interest in drinking - you can take it or leave it.
- Your confidence and self-esteem have improved.
- Your relationships no longer suffer as a result of your drinking.

- Your psychological and physical health has improved.
- Your depression has lifted.
- Your liver function has improved.

You are cured, because your brain has been restored to the condition it was in before you took that first drink. Other than total abstinence, The Sinclair Method is the only other known cure for alcoholism.

Appendix C

Helpful Resources

Bayside Community Church   **www.mybayside.church**

Bayside Community Church has developed a Growth Track consisting of the following sessions:

- My Bayside is an opportunity to know God as we gain an understanding of how our church is structured and a little of its history.

- My Family is about finding life-giving relationships in small groups.

- My Freedom is designed to encourage communication with God, recognizing His voice and walking in the freedom that comes from a relationship with Holy Spirit.

- "My Purpose" is an opportunity to learn what purpose God has for our lives, given the talents and passions He has gifted us and to help us fulfill that purpose.

  We understand that many churches are now providing similar growth opportunities for their members.

Association of Related Churches – Find a church similar to Bayside near you at **www.arcchurches.com/**

Denise Shick Her ministries include:
Help 4 Families Ministries which reaches out to families and loved ones with gender confusion issues

Living Stones Ministries which helps individuals with same sex and relational brokenness.
www.help4families.com
and **www.livingstonesministries.org**

The God I Never Knew, by Robert Morris, - Waterbrook Press

Nine O'clock in the Morning, by Dennis Bennett, - Bridge-Logos

Blue Like Jazz, By Donald Miller, - Thomas Nelson

The Cure for Alcoholism, by Roy Eskapa
Website with information about the Sinclair method
www.the-sinclair-method.com